Achromatic

Achromatic

Andrea Gardia

Illustrations by Kat Pickford

Published in Great Britain in 2024
by InkFolio Publishing House

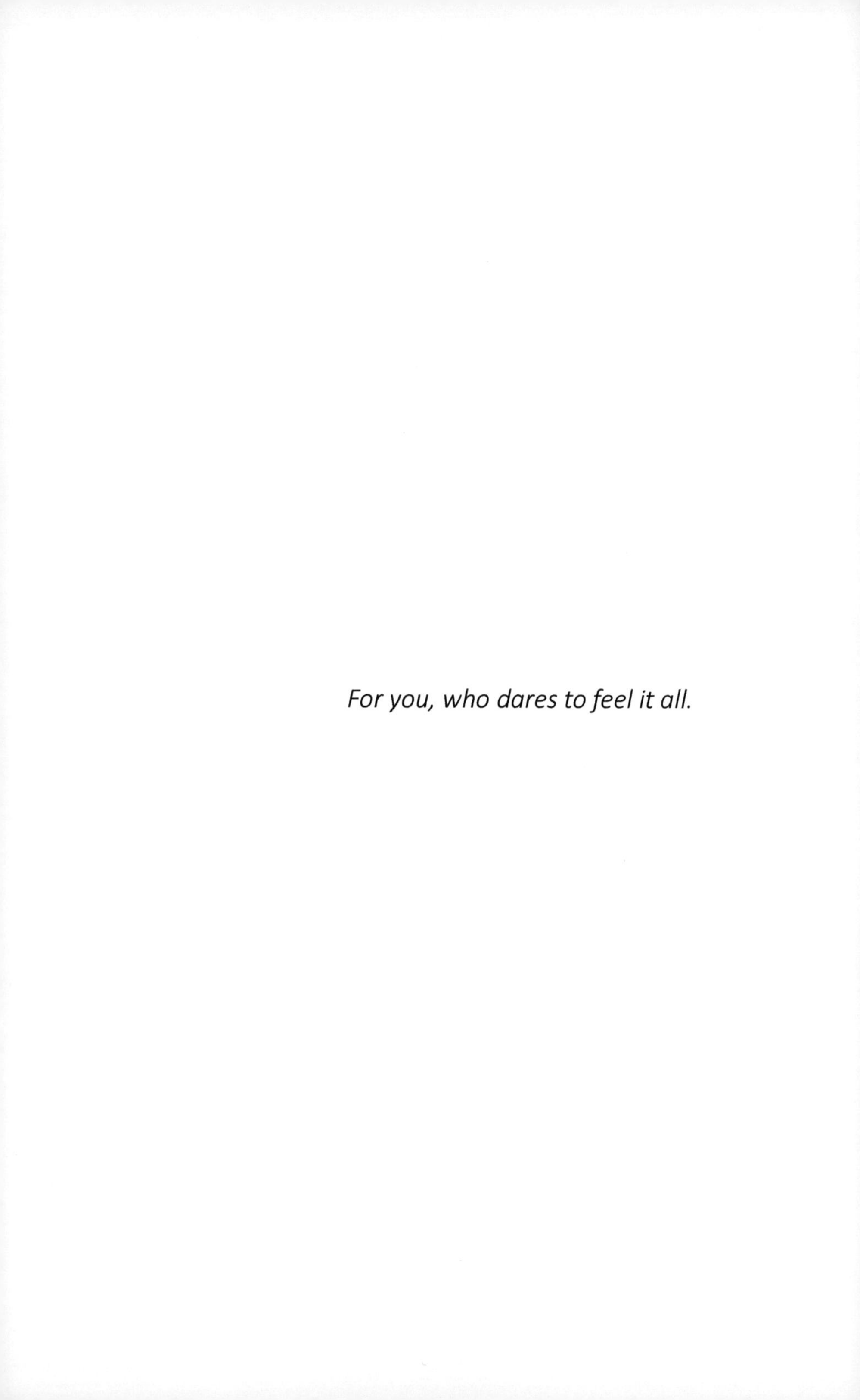

For you, who dares to feel it all.

Contents

Vows

I have made so many promises to myself that I cannot keep track of which ones I have honoured and which ones I have reneged on. Since I can remember, I've been taught to grow into a woman who will find her other half, culminating her path in marriage—promising to my beloved everything that I can't promise myself: written and overthought vows that will unite us forever until death do us part.

But now, as I sit alone with an overly bitter coffee, I write down every promise I want to keep for who should be the most important in my life: me.

I heard that you become what others need you to be,
you'll be brave if you feel someone else's fear,
you'll be certain if you are next to someone unsure,
you'll be the voice of reason in a world of madness.

You will be a badge of strength
because it is what you are expected to be,
because it is what the world wants you to be,
because it is what I need you to be.

And I, in return, will be your faded memory,
the voice of hope that tells you that you can make it,
the hand you can hold when everything else is
trembling,
that one steady refuge
always there, although not always present.

And giving you every piece of my heart,
I promise that I will talk to you and take care of you
in a way that heals and doesn't hurt.

Whenever you are ready.
Whenever the time is right.

Porcelain doll

I find myself reliving my night terrors when I daydream; it's like I am determined to make myself miserable, and whilst I wallow in my self-pity, I pray no one sees me, I pray no one else pities me.

I have a selection of paint in my wardrobe, and I relentlessly colour myself in the brightest tones as if there is no face that I cannot wear. Sometimes, against my will, the truth will shine through the cracks, and I will become, yet again, a fragile, faceless porcelain doll.

I find myself at the receiving end of all the "You look tired" and "Are you okay?". The main difference is that I now follow no templates but my own. Now, I stand tall and respond, "I am not okay". Now, I stand tall and recite this ferocious pledge that has been carved into my soul:

I have always been told:
    "It's okay not to be okay",
    "To not know what to do with yourself",
    "To be so lost, no one can find you".
And it might be okay, but it hurts.
It aches down my throat like a burning fire
that settles in my stomach and heart
and burns me slowly from the inside out,
leaving nothing but fear and ash.

I seek refuge in the past,
surrounded by a false sense of protection,
recreating the good moments
that I know will never come back.

And entangled with my future,
I've also created a utopia where I laugh again,
and my fingertips type out all the bright things
of a life I hope to live one day.

Because if it is okay to be this bad,
there must be a way to get better.

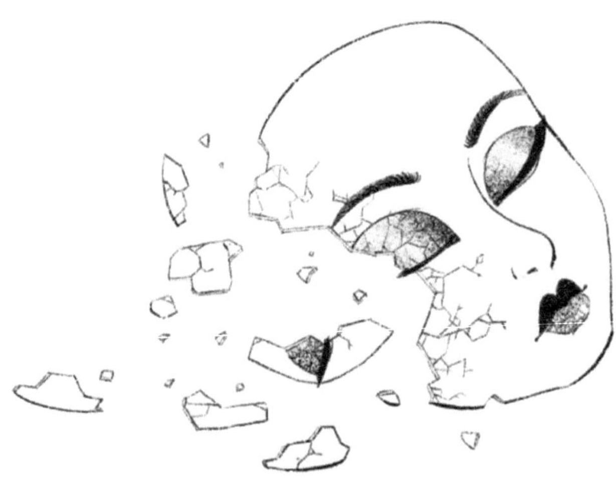

An inward war

I look in the mirror and feel things I don't understand. I look in the mirror, hoping to see all the versions of myself that I dreamt of when I was playful and young: the mathematics teacher, the violinist, the princess or the lady who cuts your hair. I look in the mirror, and I speak to myself, expecting to hear in my own echo a fitful response:

The reflection in your mirror is no longer you.
You touch, you grab, you pull.
You scar your skin, trying to find who you used to be.
And you cry, you shout, you yield.

Stop.
Breathe.

It's true...
The reflection in your mirror is no longer you.
You touch, you grab, but you let go.

You kiss your skin,
trying to make peace with who you are.
And you cry, you shout, but you defy.

Hope(less)

I have painted my skin red with brush strokes of anger and passion; I have masked myself in happiness yellow, running carelessly from what scares me, unfriending caution. When the mood is right, I will dress in prideful purple, trying to build up the courage to be more orange, full of vitality and enthusiasm... but mostly, I feel the greyness of a stormy day, full of blue slowly forfeiting its colour. But like the storms, so I shall pass.

Nothing feels worth it,
and words have lost all meaning,
people become shadows,
trapped in me, screaming.

Before I know it, the night is here,
I become one with my mind
and I question my existence:
I just want to disappear.

And I promise myself,
tomorrow will be better:
no more storms in my head,
sadness doesn't last forever.

Mirrors

I have never been able to look at myself in public mirrors;
I fear the reflection will show what I am always trying to
hide, maybe a fearful tear that's bungee jumping ropeless
for the first time, maybe the wrong kind of shimmer in my
eyes... I've never been able to look at myself in the mirrors
in my house, frightened I'll pay attention to the
imperfections deep-rooted in the self-hatred where I
often lie.

I place the mirrors a little high,
hoping I'll catch a glimpse
of the seasides and rainforests
where I imagine I could be.

I place the mirrors a little high
so the shadows can meet the light
in the dance of the reflections
creating a love story full of bright.

I place the mirrors a little high,
so it's harder for me to see
myself constantly reminding me
of who I am yet to be.

The truth is…
I always place the mirrors higher than they should be:
because I am afraid of catching
the reflection of the weak.

Make-believe

Still, tranquil, serene, quiet, peaceful, undisturbed, calm.
Seven words to evoke one emotion. Seven words to
unsettle the chaos in which I thrive.
Disarray, confusion, mayhem, madness, havoc, entropy,
lawlessness. Seven words to describe how I feel and see
myself every time I close my eyes.

I close my eyes because it hurts to see
that I don't know who I am.
I close my eyes to find myself inside
a head full of voices, all screaming at once
asking me for directions and advice on how to be calm.

Calm?- I reply with mockery- who am I to know,
if I travel to where I was never
part of and never born
Calm...? I say, full of thought
whilst I reach deep into my heart
and realise I cannot remember
the last time that I felt calm.

Is it a reality?
Is it a mental state?
Is it a game that grown children
have forgotten how to play?

I close my eyes, and I'm in darkness,
but I can finally see:
There is no arrow in this compass:
How do I set myself free?

I heart you

I heart you
in a vulnerable yet honest way
how you know you will get all your presents early
because I can't keep it contained
how you know I will always ask you
if you want a cup of tea
even if I know the answer is no
just to make you feel included and not alone.

I heart you
in a simple yet very complicated way
how I will be more hurt by you
than I will by others:
the same cut but different pain.

I heart you
and I will also forgive you sooner
because I can't stay angry at you in vain.

I heart you
Three words, two people, one flame.

1% battery

Today when I woke up
I didn't feel like moving,
it felt as if gravity pulled me down
at the edge of a timeless void, now burning.

And I look around, tired and worn,
wondering to myself where everything went wrong,
and there is no moment in time,
no wicked event that turned me,
just my busy mind and the crimes that were forced on me.

Crimes not always committed
but always thought through
intrusive thoughts that tell me, in secret,
who is the real you.

Someone to love and someone to fear,
someone to follow and someone to run away from,
someone who cares deeply about her peers,
and someone who, only alone,
can find peace in this world.

Miles

I've been walking for miles
and the orange in the trees mock me
they show me that time is passing fast
whilst I am passing through this town slowly.

The wind cherishes its beauty,
with its newfound cool breeze
and teasing dresses, for most a bounty,
makes the shore retreat back at sea.

All the miles that have been walked
can never fully be counted
and all the people earthbound and ghost
will request back the time never for accounted.

What a game to grow old,
when nothing around is growing,
the unfairest game this world-
plays with us, without us knowing.

Safety manual

I believe life should come with a safety manual:

1) Do not confuse falling in love with simply falling
   as often they hurt just the same.

2) Do not make promises when you are happy
   as when the time goes,
   so will your flame.

3) Do not spill the tea unless you are ready to clean it,
   as the stain that will remain will draw blood,
   even if you don't mean it.

4) Do not stay angry inside,
   as it will build up and grow,
   until you are left with no sight.

5) Do not tease the fire with water,
   or the gossip in your mouth
   will be our ticket to the slaughter.

6) Do not run away,
   if you do not know what you are running away from,
   the answer is not at the end of a race,
   the answer is the person that you can become.

I love you more

When I say I love you more...
I don't mean that I love you more than you love me;
I mean that I love you more than I hate our arguments,
I mean that I love you more than I did this morning
and a little less than I will tomorrow.
I mean that I love you more
than I do our "quality time",
although it is a close second.
I mean that I love you more
than it annoys me how messy you are.

And I am reminded of it
every time I pick up your dirty mugs
with the stale and dried-up tea at the bottom;
and I am reminded of it every time you are a Thursday
always in the middle, always in the way.

But I love you more than any of it bothers me.
So, when I say I love you more...
please don't say that I don't.

Because I do.

I always will.

Ssshhh!

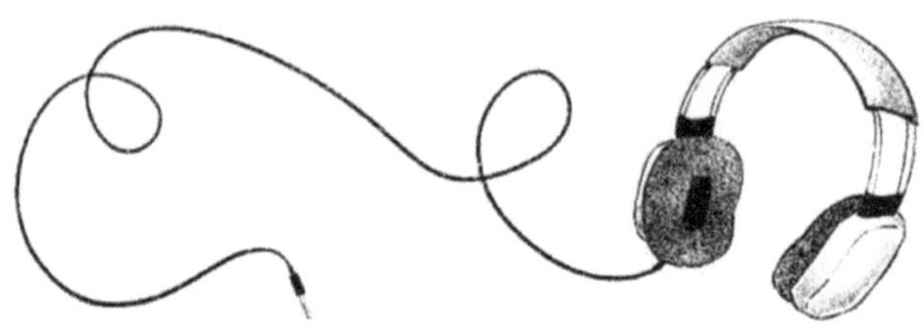

Sometimes, I wear my headphones with nothing playing to disconnect myself from myself and from everything. I avoid small talk and broken conversations, and in my muteness, I find peace.

I feel like
my soul has lost its voice
and I can no longer feel it.

There is no beat, no pulse,
just a silent rhythm.

A song that can't be sung,
and a fire that's not burning.
A scar that will not heal,
a dance without its music.

Achromatic

Is it better to never see colour or to see it with all its
brightness until, one day, there is no longer a difference
between a crowded city and a shipless sea?

To dream and to live scares me,
the memories blend with the loud voices
and they have a playdate in my head-
I can no longer distinguish either,
nor understand what has been said.

To feel pain and to die scares me,
as if your judgment met my shame
and they both merged in my head-
until I couldn't comprehend either,
nor anything I've ever said.

What is happening to me?
When did I get so lost that I can no longer find me?
Happiness doesn't feel like happiness;
sadness doesn't feel like sadness.
I know my dark places are brighter now,
but everything is the same damn colour.

Photographs

Someone called my attention
so I would strike a pose,
to immortalise a split second
for when our memory goes.

A photograph that'll become a memento
forever kept in resin and gold;
but in the time the camera shot the photo,
I was caught with my eyes closed.

A second that feels like nothing
but felt like everything underneath my skin
when I started to enumerate
all the parts of me I'd like to get rid.

I thought of all the diets and workouts
all the wonder shakes and the pills;
I felt the shame quietly winning
whilst asking myself: "Is it just me?"

Unboxing

I don't know if I am a collection of all the things that I
chose to be moving forward or if I am a collection of all
the things that I have been up until now- maybe I am
neither, maybe I am both. Maybe, I can be a beautiful
contradiction made from pain and towards healing;
maybe I am too full of packing chips that I have no space
left to be.

I am a box of stories
that I can't quite begin to tell
I am a box of stories
with a pretty top for you to unveil.

Why won't you open the box
and see what's inside?
The truth is I don't judge you...
I couldn't do it if I tried.

Inside the box, there are many things,
amongst it all a collection of untold stories-
oh! The bleeding words made their escape,
losing letters in each territory where they fell.

Inside the box, there are many things,
not only memories of pets and glory:
Written shreds made of all my wishes
and unheard voices carrying all I never said.

Inside the box, there are many things,
not only leftover cake from the parties.
There is a young girl dancing on a seaside
made from the bottles she drank to escape.

Why won't you open the box
and see what it's inside?
Am I just a collection of the pain
that I tell myself is not real
-whilst smiling
even though it's in vain?

Why won't you open the box
and see what's inside of me?
Am I just a reflection of your pain
that you tell yourself is not real
-whilst smiling
even though it's in vain?

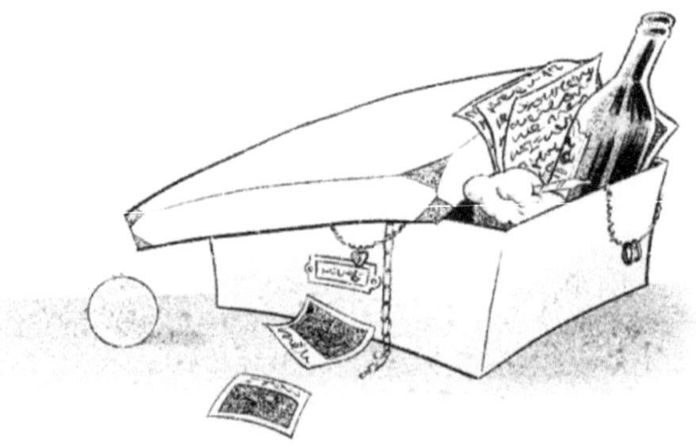

Self-destruction

"I am destroying myself so other people can't," she said,
"and it's the worst kind of control, but it's the only form I
know."

— Sue Zhao

Suddenly, the words fell out of her mouth,
and her throat tightened at the thought of speaking.
How to make sense of the unsaid
when letters have lost all meaning?

She'd been alone for a while,
faking upward progression and self-love,
filling the spaces in her bed
with loud music and tragic thoughts.

At night, the spark in her eyes dimed out
and the burning sound spread on her skin;
her fingertips stretched out,
but there was nothing for her to reach.

She curled up in the furthest corner of her immensity
hoping no one would find her broken and lost;
she feels safer and somewhat protected
if at least she remains alone.

And in the emptiness of silence,
where you can't hear her muzzled screams,
she covered the vastity of her existence
with a heartless veil carrying her dreams.

Intertwined

I've got something to confess
something that once grew within me
and then never truly left
something buried in marriage proposals
and the non-answers you always gave.

Something real hidden in the sandy rocks
where you were the x that marked the spot
when you held me tightly in your arms,
and allowed me to see you as a treasured charm.

I loved the idea of you before I met you,
and if you believe in destiny and signs
I think I was meant to find you
at the end of your shadow and the beginning of mine.

And the second I met you, I first saw your smile
hidden in your shyness and the books in your bag
I started reading all the verses of your life
hoping you'd save a chapter where I could plant my flag.

You started talking, and my world stopped
we became inseparable pieces of a jigsaw unsolved
and everything around us just started fitting
two wolves inked in this quilt I'm knitting.

The power of hindsight will always baffle me
like a joke that's not funny until it is
I once was your misinterpreted lover
I am now and forever your favourite summer.

Summers where the sun is high
and the temperature melts your pores
the summers that sometimes leave
but always return to shore.

The power of hindsight increased the power of us
forever connected, forever one fire burning two flames
forever a shining bond of two sisters
that became family after being friends.

Life to live

Your life is not yours to touch,
your life is the people you leave behind you,
and everything you mean to them.

Your life is not yours to touch,
is yours to live.

So, leave it.

Weightless

From sunrise to sundown,
she follows the footpaths through the gates
and smelling the grass, she allows a tear
to remind her of the years that await.

She sees a mare teaching her foal
to be tall in height and full of spirit
to relentlessly chase the Gaelic winds
but never crossing the limit.

She sees the sheep and the cattle,
and although she knows it's work
something within her rattles
to live just to produce, or be the produce,
to live unaware of the upcoming battle.

But alas, she returns to the cottage
with dirty hands and a heavy heart
and when she looks at the scale, it marks zero
showing the weightlessness of her acts.

Standing still

I've given up everything that I am. I have put down the knife and packed away my sins; I have bathed in salts that revived my skin, and I have closed my eyes as I sunk in. And I stand still, although I am barely standing to shout at myself that this fight is worth fighting. I beg myself to clean my wounds and try again; I beg myself to remember that I am not alone in this life that sometimes feels like hell.

I can't run forever
there are things I can't escape:
my thoughts, my nightmares,
the voices in my head.
The moments of my past,
I so fondly remember
and the ones I block out,
and wish to forget.

I can't run forever,
I need to freeze time,
stand still until I know me
appreciate what I have.
The bright moments and the sunshine
the pleasantness of bathing at sea,
the memories I am creating,
the drawn details on my skin.

It's not always about running,
about hiding from what I am;
is also about accepting,
that I changed, and it won't last.

Dualities

A battle between the light and the dark,
a struggle that shines through,
needless to say,
the eyes of painted troubles without a spark.

What a price to pay for the tediousness of breathing,
loveless pieces lost amidst the fight,
more turmoil and stronger power
more protection from its birth-given right.

To wish both good and perverse,
to vanish when the sun rises and sets,
how mistaken have generations been,
bound to rules ripping through our skin.

Light and dark, once sworn enemies
now, bathe together and laugh
in the purity of the duality of endings
of the stories that never did quite start.

Whispers

The whispers in my mind tell me I'm not whole
they tell me I've lost it all amidst an imaginary battle
they tell me I'll never find my pieces nor be at peace.
There is no route to lead me home.

The whispers in my head have formed an alliance
they tell me everybody sleeps whilst I lie awake
they tell me everybody lies to get ahead in the games
games of war played by growling growing children.

And I really thought I could fight them off
when I dressed myself in a suit of armour
covering my heart and my toes
whilst marching at the beat of the fire.

Insomnia

Another night filled with insomnia
that reminds me of the emptiness in my heart
looking up at the night sky
hoping to find a guiding star.

There is a slight breeze
that nurses me back and forth
just to steal the coveted rest
I've been hoarding for so long.

I look down to the ground
but I see no hell shining through
because the sour truth of my existence,
is that hell lives within my runes.

Runes of a past that I seem to constantly remember,
and a future so fragile I'm not strong enough to build,
runes of all my past selves gathered in December,
feeling hopeful that I'm alive, even thrilled.

And I catch a glimpse of my reflection in the window
and briefly blinded, I see who I could be,
but it quickly vanishes, leaving me hopeless
returning to my present: tired, awake and restless.

Footsteps

I followed the footsteps on the sand,
hoping they would lead me to you
and after walking for three miles
I realised we've always been one split in two.

What happened to the hopefulness?
What happened to the bond?
When did we become so restless
that we don't recognise who we've become?

I followed the footsteps on the sand,
hoping they would lead me to you,
wishing you would be waiting on a boat,
so together, we could sail through.

You are the forever shining lighthouse
at the end of a sail and through a stormy night.
You are the light that guides me
when there is nothing left of me to guide.

Bloody red flags

Bloody red flags that no one should accept
with the abrasive and abusive pinned down and held
acrimonious dates with a belligerent undertone
running away, deceitfully, not answering the phone.

How can they be so egotistical and jealous?
It is a litigious fact how they find love.
I can't believe how obnoxious they are,
with their opportunistic get-ups and deplorable hearts.

Petty and tyrannical, these unfaithful, fallacious beings
their abominable acts, immoral, empty of meaning
an incompetent grown-up child, ignorant and vile
clueless on what love should be like, do not smile.

I hope you don't accept it; don't become complicit
they are guilty of negligence; love is not implicit.
If they treat you with contempt
and take you for granted;
remind them, you are worth it;
don't become enchanted.

They should feel guilty for being disgraceful
if their company is a synonym for painful.
No forgiveness is given to the abusive partner:
Let's all be smarter- close off that chapter.

Treasure hunt

On this journey of self-awareness, I realise that there are moments where free will is a utopia I cannot reach; some things are meant to happen, some things were always meant to be - and so I play along with my inner child, and I allow her to feel seen and safe.

It's all about running:
to run free, catching up to the future;
to run wild, enjoying the uneven ride;
to run aimlessly, looking for myself.

It's all about running:
Who does she run with, and why?
The life she runs toward and its shine,
and how will she get there? Can she fly?

It's all about running:
to run far away from the past,
to outrun my nights of insomnia,
deciphering clues before I crash.

It's all about running:
for the biggest treasure hunt ever made,
to find myself and to be found by others,
to win, to lose, or to at least partake.

On the edge

I am the person I argue the most with, constantly jumping between starting again, embracing the freshness of a new start, and working hard on everything I have built so far. I will set arguments and counterarguments to showcase the best of both imagination-riddled worlds. Still, I will often find myself stuck in the middle, unable to reach either option until the inability to establish a course leaves me dying of thirst and hunger.

What an argument to have: live or let life live you.

The thought of life lingered in my mind,
my Dionysus's side sailed to never return
whilst I stayed grounded on known land
for when I crashed - I would not burn.

My eyes caught a roaming silhouette
and a glimpse of all the stories that had been said
I felt all the ones that were never spoken
and sunk with a weight in my chest.

I dreamt about the tightness of my arms around me,
how they held me and gave me warmth.
I dreamt about the tightness of my arms around me,
afraid it wouldn't be enough.

During a fragment in time,
I was two made into one,
I stopped the sand from falling
and began to crack all at once.

I didn't want to let go.
I would have never let go.

But-
Chose to say goodbye and stand by it,
decided to close the door and throw away the key,
chose safe, chose known, chose right,
determined to live my already-made life.

Devil behind the door

The dark seas and the dark minds,
they both allure me the same
and I wish I wasn't enchanted by the murk
consuming me and stealing my name.

It is the devil that's coming to get me,
waiting behind the unlocked door,
he knows I won't be able to close it
once he lets himself in ready for war.

There is nowhere that I can run,
there is no place big enough to hide,
the malevolent frigid air surrounds me...
Will he take me, or have I already died?

He sees my eyes pouring abundant and raw fear
he sees my hands shaking and my skin pale
he caresses me gently, about to steal a kiss
a deadly kiss on a body that wasn't for sale.

And I am left soulless and marginalised,
left for dead but somehow still breathing
and he doesn't know that he's awoken in me
a rising anger in this heart seething.

Unspoken truths

I have known no soul able to speak freely about all their
troubles; there is always one truth knotted up, unable to
become sound, and the more it remains unspoken, the
more it hurts to think about, and the easier it is to bury
under 100 feet of doubt.

Your mind will always go to your secret place,
to your most desired hiding spot
and will rest there-
from everything and everyone.

Your body, tired of the expectations of living,
will merge with the ground
and will rest there-
from everything and everyone.

But you will keep bleeding, in silence,
arguing with your thoughts
telling yourself that you can fight this- alone,
and because you hurt, you hurt others.

Find "that" someone you can rest with and trust,
clean your wounds and stop the bleeding- in silence.

Because we are all healing from something
that we can't talk about.

Clock watching

There is a certain beauty in watching life elapse before your eyes whilst everyone else is resting, and when morning comes, everyone chases the lost hours; the alarm clocks never sleep in, and the ones asleep never actually wake up.

Tick-Tock...
Tick-Tock...
My eyelids feel heavy,
trying to close up on me,
I'm exhausted from living
but I cannot sleep.

Tick-Tock...
Tick-Tock...
My body is pinned to the ground,
but my thoughts are running wild.
I'm here, I'm there,
I am nowhere to be found.

My eyelids will turn into water
whilst my skin turns into sand,
and I stand still inaudible,
shouting that my freedom-
                    is not mine.

Rainy day

A warm coffee for a cold heart,
an old book that smells like history,
to empty myself from myself
and fill my mind with fantasy.

A cosy spot next to a rainy window,
and a dim light that fills my dreams,
a memory that I can barely remember,
who I am and who I used to be.

Lines

I am not who I was yesterday, and I am not who I will be tomorrow. My heart beats towards the unknown, and you can see it in my eyes. The world keeps spinning, and I just need it to stop. I need to catch my breath and return to the present.

To accept any change is hard,
you stand in front of yourself
vulnerable like ever
and you draw a line.

A line that separates
what is with what it was,
that goes around your present
and holds you in the past.

That line is not straight,
that line is barely a line,
that line is your efforts to keep normality
under a norm you never liked.

No voices but one

She was worried her body couldn't hold her heart. She was worried that she had too much inside of her and that it would all explode, destroying everything and everyone around her. Because why wouldn't it? It has been close to destroying herself on a few occasions.

Loud head and fuzzy thoughts,
floating through the motions of her own flaws
driving and being driven, abiding social laws
and if she breaks, she breaks alone
whether she drowns or stays afloat.

She says there are no voices in her head- but one
it judges and shouts and questions, tortures and rattles
she shushes it,
hoping the quiet will help with the busyness of her mind
but the truth is, there aren't any voices but one.

Her own voice as a different persona,
her own personal brand of kryptonite,
her own voice always familiar yet always distant
becoming a bully who feasts on fears and cries.

When did she become so fearful of herself?
Was there so much kindness given to others that there
was none left?
How to stop the vicious cycle, if there is even a way?
She wants to be healthy and stable and live a life without
being afraid.

So, she waits another day, hoping the fog will clear
hoping she will be able to think without
that dissenting voice corrupting her tired being,
either die or let her die- as she knows well...
Hell is real.

Empty

I got my notebook out,
and my favourite pen,
and I thought I'd write everything I was feeling.

I waited,
for the words to start pouring out,
but the page remained blank.

After a while, I realised I could not have said it better
myself:

Empty.

Goodbye

I will become a distant yet cherished memory, one that you will not always remember but that you will always keep. The truth is that I have never been good at goodbyes. I fear you will try to stop me, and we'll both get emotional, and I'll cry. I've never been too good at goodbyes, leaving whilst unnoticed through the back door, avoiding your eyes.

The day had been filled
with sunshine in her head
and heavy clouds in her heart.

She'd been wanting to say goodbye;
goodbye to the silent corridors,
she'd filled with laughter and runs,
goodbye to the narrated stories
and to the ones she never told,
goodbye to the people and the sadness and the love,
goodbye to everyone's everything
- she wanted herself gone.

As the day passed, silence overshadowed presence,
the unsaid was burning on the tip of their tongues-
unpaired letters lost for words.
She was going to be gone, no takebacks, no hope.

Whilst her surroundings were gasping for air,
she turned as light as a summer breeze,
she whispered goodbye and flew away with her wings;
she held her head up high and abandoned past beliefs.

And as the clock ticked the end of another tedious day,
there was no her, no memory, no trace;
she camouflaged with the shadows of the unimportant...
Was she ever... truly there?

I never let her out

Trained.
Conditioned.
Taught.
To take every punch and swallow my own blood.

The rage, screaming, hitting,
having my surroundings collapse.
Yet,
I am still, calm,
as if unfaced by it all.

I never let her out,
the child that argues back,
the child that cries until there is no sound left
but the one of the tears hitting the ground.

I never let her out,
when I want to make everything around me
fly to its own crash;
when I want to draw blood,
and list all the pain I've been hoarding inside.

I never let her out,
because if it comes down to a duel till death,
I know I will have drawn my very last breath.

Dry blood

My heart has lost its voice
and I can no longer feel it.

There is no beat, no pulse
just a silent rhythm.

A song that can't be sung
and a fire that's not burning.

A scar that will never heal,
from a wound no longer hurting.

Out of place

Like a shell in the middle of a forest,
like a song without a beat,
like these feelings I keep down under,
my biggest, most painful deceit.

When the shape of you doesn't fit the space you are in,
and time is an illusion you've forgotten to check,
when you've become your own shadow
with fear and doubt wrapped around your neck.

There is no place you should take,
there is no race you need to win,
there are no mistaken moments,
only memories etched on your skin.

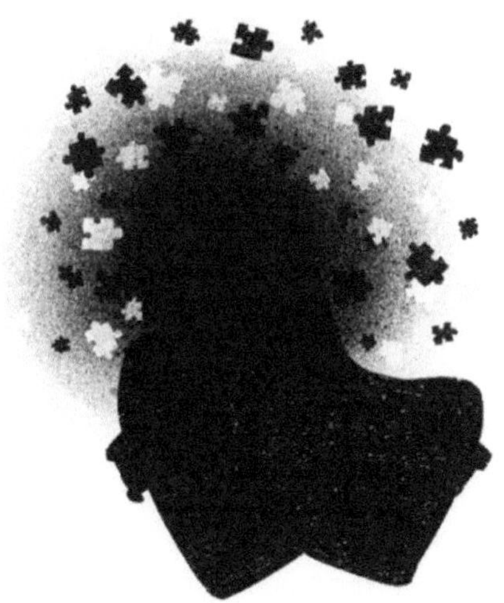

Poetic suicide

Her eyelids felt heavy every time her mind emptied the tears held hostage in her heart, feeling scared that once out, it would flood her entire self. Her hands, in pain from the thoughts carried out by the devil, became two snakes wrapped around her neck, depriving her of the very breath that kept her alive.

What a shameful way to die: alone and in silence
where neither blood nor sweat nor tears leave a mark.
What a shameful way to die: hidden in your own mind
where the cries for help remain uncried,
forgotten in the dark.

She knew she'd come too far,
ripping herself from the inside out.
Viscerally,
she encountered her most tortured self and asked:
How can you just stand there
and watch me burn alive?
How can you just stand there?
Do you know I won't survive?

Depict of life, she lied down and began to accept:
The nonsensical journey of the lost
was never to be found
because if it can get better, it can get worse
the same foolish story

with its meaning never said aloud.
No arrows left in the quiver,
even though no arrows were ever shot,
lost in the journey towards the ever-after
tempting fate with blood.
What a stupid thing to do,
to brave the elements in battle,
what a profanity it is to shout:
Hurrah to the dead in their soulless travel!

The pain turned into anger,
and so, this turned into despair
the memories that chased her,
what a blasphemy to play fair,
from the hair, she was pulled back
now staring directly up above
wishing the end of it all with a slice across her throat.

Drained of life, her eyelids no longer felt heavy.
Empty, she fell onto the ground
mimicking a colour-changing leaf,
she was no longer spellbound.
The soil welcomed a no longer fearing self
as the gift that she'd always been
and embraced her remains, a heart no longer beating
so the rest could finally begin.

Kintsugi

I have a surge of life pouring out, and I cannot recognise
the poor soul that gambled with the devil for a night of
rest. I have swum in an oasis made of gold, and the
shadows can no longer wound me with their words. I will
forever be as broken as I am whole.

They say time heals all wounds;
and angry, I curse time.
They told me to be patient and wait,
and I asked: for what?

For my coffee to go cold,
for the days to be shorter,
for me to be too old,
or for an unlived life to end?

For my memories to fade,
for the moon to not wake up,
for the pain and sadness to hug me,
or for my body to give up?

There is no time to feel sorry,
there is no time for dead words-
If it's meant to be, make it happen,
you can set your own course.

You have been living a lie,
no trail, no dream, no hope;
but it's time you see the lighthouse,
raise the mainsail, find your north.

There is a storm inside you,
there has been one for a while,
the water will overfill your sorrow,
I beg you, let it all out.

There is a storm inside you,
there has been one for a while,
use the wind to guide you,
reach the shore, embrace your land.

Holding onto hope

Hi,
I trust this email finds you well.

I've been thinking about you,
I've been writing every day,
Yet... there is still so much to say.

How my sleepless nights and sleepy days
have filled my weeks;
How the sunsets and the sunrises
no longer taste the same;
and how, for the first time,
I decided to lose my shoulders
so I didn't have to carry the weight.

How my birthday had a sour undertone,
and how my soul is ripped between
living like there is no tomorrow
and wishing there wasn't one at all.
How I miss you when you are gone,
and how you tire me relentlessly when you are present...
Yet please... please don't go.

Don't go... because
without you, I turn to sand,
and my bones turn to ash,
and my mind becomes haunted

with the ghosts of my past.
So please... please... don't go
because my heart can't bear it.

The world slowly implodes
and there isn't a soul in sight to tell me
that it's okay when you are gone
because I don't talk about you;
that's it's okay if I forget you
because I simply don't want to;
that it's okay to let you go
when I cannot fathom releasing the rope
that's digging and cutting through my skin
to the point of grinding into my bones.

So please... please don't go,
because there is no one I would believe but you.

So, I beg you, please don't go
Because without you,
I might lose it all.

Sorry I went on for so long.
Should you need me or should there be anything I can do
for you, please don't hesitate to ask.
My contact details are below.

Yours sincerely,
Andrea

Printed by Libri Plureos GmbH in Hamburg, Germany